THE COMMUNAL FAMILY

Model for Change

THE COMMUNAL FAMILY

Model for Change

STEVE BRIDGE

LOQUAT PRESS
Berkeley, California

ISBN 0-9631099-0-1
Library of Congress Catalog Card Number 488-276

Copies may be ordered from
Loquat Press
P.O. Box 11507
Berkeley, CA 94701

Designed by Sara Glaser
Illustrated by Laura E. Fisher

Printed by
Inkworks, a collective
Berkeley, California

printed on recycled paper

This book is dedicated to recovering the ownership and control of Planet Earth from the prodigals and restoring it to all creatures including the human family. Once we lived in communal family groups where our instincts for sharing, learning, and consensus flourished, and where the earth was owned in common. But this paradise was destroyed by an ambitious minority of greedy, power-hungry males.

It is a paradise that we can finally begin to regain.

Acknowledgment

I am not a writer and have never really been a writer. When I was eighteen and a freshman at Wesleyan University in 1925, I found myself with a severe case of writer's block. I knew how to write, but was in such psychological turmoil that I could not put pen to paper. Now, some 67 years later, I find that the words flow from me, but not always in the right order. Thus in producing this book I have been helped by the editing and ghost writing of two men, Tim Beneke and Chuck Stephen. They have taken my ideas, filtered them through their own common sense, and expressed them in ways that most readers should be able to understand. In addition, I owe a strong debt to Minnie Favre and Patrick Haggarty for their editing work and many helpful suggestions.

While I have been on a long intellectual journey the last few years that has taken me through many books and ideas, I feel that the greatest source of my understanding has been my eighty-five years of living and struggling to make sense of the world. I believe that American society has fallen upon very hard times and that the greatest imperative of any book should be to offer us a path out of our desperate condition. That is what I have tried to do. If others build upon my ideas, or make sense of them to experiment with new forms of communal living, then I shall have accomplished my task.

Contents

Prologue

In what follows I offer both a critical glimpse of the past and a visionary model of the future. My aspiration has been to ascertain a pivotal wrong turn that humanity once took, and to suggest a new path that will restore us to a state of both material and spiritual well being.

Some ten thousand years ago human societies witnessed the emergence of prodigal sons—oppressive, domineering men—who abandoned the reigning egalitarian spirit and began to dominate their fellow humans. Such prodigals have forced us to live by animal instincts and to repress what is best in human nature.

What is a prodigal? He or she is someone in whom the ancient instinct for group living, learning, and sharing has atrophied and given way to selfishness and a taste for easy and immediate pleasure. Stripped of instinctual guidance, the prodigal arrogantly lives without a home or direction. Neither contributing to nor supported by the human family, he zigzags through life in hopeless pursuit of his shifting and insatiable wants.

The prodigal, whether he knows it or not, is sick. He seeks glamour and status, for himself and not for the common good. He discovers that these rewards do not quench his thirst, they only cause him to demand more and more.

The prodigal sickness can be difficult to perceive because it is so common and familiar, like the atmosphere we breathe. In politics and economics, from Wall Street to Hollywood, the prodigals stamp their values onto the nation. By forming families and passing down their genes, they threaten to go even further, not only defining our culture but reshaping human nature down to its core. For this reason, to protect the human gene, we must recover the communal family form as rapidly as we can.

Human life has been dominated by hierarchies that have brought us environmental destruction and the threat of nuclear peril. We have wrongfully assumed that the hierarchial structure common among animals predisposes humans toward hierarchy and competition. What is truly natural for humans is consensus and cooperation.

I dream of a future in which humans live in small villages comprised of communal family groups who work together in collectively run and owned businesses. In such a world people would work four hours a day, and devote the rest of their time to education, playing with their children, and enjoying the arts. It is in the service of this dream that I have written this book.

COMMON SENSE

Common sense teaches us that we need a new understanding of families. Human families must have four basic rights.

1. Each child is conceived only with the consensus of the entire communal family.
2. Human beings, like all creatures, are free to create for themselves shelters of good quality.
3. Land is owned not by landlords but by everyone. The fields, forests, mountains, and meadows all are part of nature. Even the land under our cities—our homes, offices, factories, and roads, our parking lots, condos, apartment buildings, and shopping malls—is for all humankind to use and enjoy.
4. No one controls others. We rely on inborn common sense, not force, to create the consensus our instincts call for. All

persons are created equal and no one ought to work as the servant of another.

In the past children's rights have been monopolized by males. But they should rest in communal groups and the human instinct for consensus.

Sometimes intellectuals use their intellects to complicate what ought to be very simple. The mind is a wonderful servant but a poor master. When it is used to say more and more about less and less, the mind creates problems rather than solving them. We get so involved examining a single tree that we lose sight of the forest.

This point is made very well by E.J. Applewhite in his book *Paradise Mislaid.* Applewhite was concerned to answer a basic question, "What is life?" He spent five years foraging through books and journals trying to find an answer to his question. What he found was that the most esteemed scientists and thinkers could do no better than common sense. In fact they frequently did worse.

Common sense, says Applewhite, is a part of every human being's natural endowment. It is something that does not necessarily grow greater through education. On the contrary, as the familiar stereotype of the absent-minded professor suggests, education can cause a person to lose touch with common sense. In fact, people who appear to lack great intellectual capacity sometimes have a great deal of common sense. What was most striking to Applewhite was that from a common sense perspective the questions that troubled him did not seem so difficult.

Common sense is the natural intuitive capacity of ordinary people to spontaneously make sense of reality. When Applewhite examined what scientists had to say about the mystery of life the questions grew muddier and muddier. He encountered complex and controversial analyses of the relations between molecules and consciousness. He saw life viewed from the perspective of atoms, from the perspective of evolution, even from the perspective of computers and artificial intelligence.

One of the most charming insights he encountered was one that stood reality on its head. Samuel Butler said that a hen was an egg's way of making another egg. This point has been reestablished in different ways. Biologist Edward O. Wilson claimed that an organism is only DNA's way of making more DNA. George Wald, a physicist himself, said that a physicist is only an atom's way of knowing about atoms. Life can be seen as a powerful natural force which endlessly reproduces itself. The end of life is simply to generate more life. In doing this human beings are a kind of accidental byproduct. Such a perspective puts human existence in a whimsical comic light, but it doesn't really tell us what life is.

Applewhite's conclusion is that despite these ingenious theories, humans really already know what life is. We know when someone is alive and conscious and when someone is dead to the world. We can tell when a creature has awareness and when one does not. For instance, if we look at the issue of abortion, it is evident that we do not tax or grant privileges to the unborn. We do not count pregnant women twice when we conduct a census. We already possess a common sense view of things that ought to resolve the issue of abortion for us.

It is common sense itself that ought to tell us when to rely on common sense and when we need the advice of technical experts. The academic experts, like most people, try to extend their power as much as possible, often into the domain where it doesn't apply. Applewhite's reflections are a useful corrective against this tendency.

As a matter of fact, it is common sense, not scientific theory, that has inspired and guided this book. Common sense tells us that no man created the earth, and thus no one ought to control the land or its fruits. Common sense tells us that all men are created equal and that none ought to work as the servant of another. It is common sense that tells us we ought not to despoil the earth but leave it in a state that future generations may enjoy.

Indeed this book is no more than an exercise in common sense. It is based on principles that concern all human beings and that ought to be evident to all. They are recognized by more and more people as time goes on, and ultimately will replace our present-day laws of the land.

The first of these principles is that no person shall control or dominate others, whether by force, cunning, or exploitation of the laws of supply and demand. We have abolished slavery and inherited privilege. Yet American society remains one of the most unequal on earth, allowing some people vast power over the lives of others.

The second principle is that no person should control the land, or other vital resources of the earth. The earth is not man's property but belongs to every species that dwells upon it. And the earth's fruits must be more equally shared. This is a lesson of common sense that has spread throughout the world over the past several centuries.

The third principle is that no person or group ought to control conception against the interest of mothers and children themselves. For most of history, women have been no more than vessels of conception and children no more than servants of their parents. If women were to gain a say in how their bodies are used, the population crisis would be mitigated and families would be strengthened by a spirit of love and mutual respect.

These are principles of common sense that together we must translate into practice.

Each child is conceived only with the consensus of the entire communal family.

Human beings, like all creatures, are free to create for themselves shelters of good quality.

Land is owned not by landlords but by everyone.
The fields, forests, mountains, and meadows all are part of nature.
Even the land under our cities—our homes, offices, factories,
and roads, our parking lots, condos, apartment buildings, and
shopping malls—is for all humankind to use and enjoy.

Human beings are created equal, no one a servant and no one a master. We rely on our inborn common sense, not force, to create the consensus of our instincts.

Introduction

Communal family living existed in our hunting and food gathering period and it is also our best hope for the future. Today we live in a world in which two thirds of the people are subjugated and scarcely one third free. Women are the property of men, children the property of parents, and land and its resources property for the greediest. Social relationships are often motivated by selfishness and exploitation of neighbors, and the goals of government are power, wealth and military control. We must return to our social instincts to save ourselves and our progeny from a catastrophic extinction of life on our planet earth.

Such a great revolution of values can only come about through one source, the human family itself. The sons and daughters of the prodigals, who left the family fold many centuries ago, must return and reintegrate into villages and communal family groups.

Among the aborigines of Australia, who live in communal groups, women are the caretakers of the entire tribe. They fulfill a role that allows their natural abilities to flourish and gives them a dignity which American women are denied. They pass on the traditions of the group and instill in everyone a respect for interdependence. The instinctual qualities of empathy and care, if nurtured by women in family groups, would spread through our public life as well if given a chance.

Throughout the world humans need to learn to live again in stable integrated communal family groups, which in today's world is worth more than money can buy. Communal family groups seek to balance their membership by economic class, race, gender, and educational background. Our need for this kind of life is deeply rooted in our biological and evolutionary endowment as primates. One of the benefits primates get from being social animals is that group living offers the opportunity for prolonged learning during childhood. Learning is an activity in which primates engage far more then any other animals and the purpose of learning is to equip individuals in a group with more knowledge of the environment for their survival.

The more evolved an animal, the longer the period of learning in which the offspring is dependent upon adults. Chimpanzees, our closest animal cousins, are infants and juveniles for a total of ten years before they become functioning adults. A comparison of the size of their brain to ours indicates that if chimps need ten years of nurture and learning, we need even more than that or perhaps continual learning from birth to death. But currently our society suppresses instincts for learning, which gives rise to a multitude of problems.

A good deal of primate learning, anthropologist Richard Leakey tells us, is cooperative and social. Group living and the wisdom it brings was once the basis and origin of human culture. A group of primates might together possess knowledge about places where food could be obtained that no member of the group alone would possess. Such a social organization was the basis of hunter gatherer societies until about ten thousand years ago.

In recent years detailed studies of chimpanzees have served to shed light on human behavior. We humans would like to believe that we are radically different from any other species. Most of us would probably prefer not to think of ourselves as animals at all or as having instincts. But the truth is that humans have needs that must be met and that aside from the simple biological needs of hunger and thirst, the highest human motives are like those of chimpanzees, motives for social learning.

Research by Frans DeWaal, a Dutch ethologist, suggests that if women were as free as men to follow their instincts we wouldn't have so many ignorant people nor so many problems. And our government would have no need of thousands of social workers and a massive Department of Education.

DeWaal did what no one had done before; he built a tower to study chimps in captivity more thoroughly than any had been studied before. There were nine females and four males in the group. A simple chart of their interactions reveals something interesting: the female chimps related to each other far more often and with far more flexibility than did the males. They expressed more emotions, but on the whole were also more peaceful.

This natural tendency, found in human females as well as apes, ought to be cherished and nurtured far more than it is today. Among the chimps DeWaal studied was an old female he named Mama. Mama was a virtual matriarch in the chimpanzee clan, and a conciliating force when tensions mounted among the chimps. Often two males would be in conflict and on the verge of violence; then instead of fighting, they would come rushing to Mama screaming loudly.

On one occasion Mickie, the "alpha" male or patriarch, outraged the rest of the chimps with his violent behavior. As a consequence they chased him up a tree and refused to let him come down. Mickie sat at the top of the tree, alone, panic stricken and screaming. Whenever he tried to come down some other chimps chased him back up. After a quarter hour of this, Mama slowly climbed the tree and kissed and comforted Mickie, and Mickie safely followed her down and made up with the other chimps.

If chimpanzees can have social organizations with strong females as peacemakers, why can't human beings ? Don't most women consider restriction in a nurturing role to be "slavery," just as they were saddled with the children and domestic duties in the past?

We are the only creatures who kill members of our own species as a business. Yet today research continues into more lethal methods of death and destruction. This makes no sense given our large brain, produced by millenia of cooperative learning in groups. It is part of our natures as human beings to help one another, by contributing to the group's well-being rather than being aggressive and self aggrandizing. No primate society would have survived long if it traveled the path we are presently taking.

By returning to life in communal family groups we can control our birth rate and reduce family size. Scientists have shown that in every species, including our hominid ancestors, females are the caretakers of the group. They nurture the young, care for the sick and elderly, and enhance the power of love and cooperation against forces that threaten to dissolve the group. Females also strengthen the society in a subtler and even more powerful way: they control the birth rate by instigating conception only when new babies are needed.

Thus women have the instinctual power to curb growth. But their oppression by lustful males has kept them from expressing their instincts for over 5000 years. The harmony of our instincts has been sacrificed to short-sighted greed. Only in communal family groups, where women share power and each adult depends on every other, will our dizzying birth rates finally be reduced. Reduction of our birth rate can reduce the pressure on all species threatened by extinction. It will also help our mental and emotional problems.

Fortunately, there have been many examples in human history of the communal spirit that marked our hominid ancestors. Many of these were solid successes; some flourished into the modern world.

The Shakers, to take one example, gave top priority to creativity and the entrepreneurial spirit, which they believed flourished best in communal living groups. Their craftsmanship was admired not only by everyone of that period but also by people today. The Shakers were concerned with perfecting their work, struggling with each project to achieve the highest quality and giving hardly a thought to profit. They became experts at many things. They built some of the best roads of the time and invented the washing machine and the circular saw, breakfast cereals, clothes pins and cut nails.

But the Shakers' principal achievement was their care of children. The Shakers themselves were celibate but operated a pioneering boarding school to which families from miles around brought their children to develop under Shaker influence. The children lived in dormitories separate from their parents where they were supervised by "elders" in the ways of the community. They were raised in an atmosphere where they learned to value themselves as bearers of an important tradition. There was strict equality among the children and between boys and girls. The children had plenty of healthy food, appropriate clothing, books, and playthings. In the Shaker schools, which were widely renowned, children learned that they could depend on one another and must give each other support.

Perhaps the Shakers were drawing on deep-seated instincts, ones that we have been forced to repress. What are the lessons of these communities, non-human and human, for modern men and women? It seems clear that in integrated communal families, where people live together in villages of family groups—each composed of about ten to twenty adults and their children—life would be far richer than it has ever been. The pairing off of men and women is of course natural, but this needs to be within the communal family fold and not as prodigals.

There are vestiges of community today for us to build on. In the

U.S. itself there are over 30,000 people living in communes and experimenting with the idea of sharing their lives. But in the future we can go far beyond this by gradually taking over the profit businesses of agriculture, industry, and commerce, making them less stressful and more efficient by the fact that communal families and their collective businesses need neither bureaucracy nor hierarchy. We must undertake this before time runs out.

The greed of the prodigals has moved us backwards for ten thousand years and led us to behave like those animals whose instincts force them into hierarchies. But our large brains make hierarchy unnecessary. Consensus, where hierarchy ceases to exist, will come about naturally and instinctively when we live in communal family groups.

CHAPTER 1

Prodigals Are Destroying Our Heritage of Life

The prodigals in their greed for selfish profit have exploited us for centuries. This has created a "war of all against all" that holds mankind in its bloody grip as neighbors compete against each other everywhere. Blacks are in conflict with other blacks, Arabs fight Arabs and Jewish groups argue with other Jews. All over the world, ethnic groups are struggling for their human rights. The Irish, Lebanese, and Ethiopians have been fighting civil wars for many years. And on the Indian subcontinent conflicts are almost too complex to understand.

My 85 years of experience warn me that the entire human family is on a path to complete extinction, perhaps within the lifetime of our grandchildren. We are threatened by increasing turmoil in the Middle East, in Eastern Europe and the Soviet Union. Worldwide, we face worsening pollution, runaway military spending, and a rapidly widening gulf between the rich and poor. In the background, like a ticking clock, the earth's population will double in less than forty years.

The prodigals in the U.S., like those in the Soviet Union, China, and the other nation states, are crushing us with their military hardware and stripping the human family of its talent, which is now devoted to war and not to food, shelter, or other human needs. Were industry operated under family collectives there would be no pollution of our atmosphere, no CO2 destruction of the ozone layer nor pesticide poisoning of our soil. We need a new structure of communal family groups which can create economic abundance, equality and free lifetime education for everyone. It is ignorance that brought the prodigals to power and only ignorance will keep them there. The governments and corporations of the prodigals now dominate most people's lives in ways that earlier centuries could not even imagine. Their immense bureaucracies, armed with computers, possess techniques of surveillance and propaganda that threaten the privacy of every individual and hinder the formation of every new social group. Distrust among the citizens often provides the excuse for expanding governmental control. Instead of cooperating together to help themselves, people demand that the government do more things for them. Protests and demonstrations are confused with political freedom. The propaganda of democracy causes people to believe they have influence, when in reality it is the narcissistic prodigals who control everyone's life.

The fact is, human beings everywhere are becoming greedy prodigals preying on the compassionate and cooperative people who are struggling to live. For most of history, people relied on neither government nor experts to tell them how to lead their lives. They learned to help themselves and relied on the cooperation of communal family groups. On the whole, society was held together by trust, not force.

Throughout the world, people seem to be losing the skills, awareness and ability to create consensus that are nurtured by living together in groups, where matters of interest to everyone are decided in intense, face to face discussions that breed trust. More and more—perhaps under the influence of movies and TV—they turn inward to the isolation of the nuclear family, seeking some shred of affection and respect otherwise denied them by the impersonal organizations that govern the world. Whereas the communal family group constantly teaches and educates, the nuclear family is a social shipwreck. It focuses its members narrowly on the present, limits their love and understanding to one other person, fixates their duties to children who are their own, and separates them from the great sweep of human history and time.

The prodigals' oligarchies are expanding their control of the world with multinational organizations that portend a new totalitarianism, one that directs all facets of everyone's life. Such impersonal bureaucracies escape responsibility as did the Nazis in Hitler's Germany. Each bureaucrat just does what he is told to do. The natural groupings of families, neighborhoods, villages and guilds have either disappeared or are in decay. Longing for the trust and cooperativeness that such groups inspired, individuals feel lonely, isolated and helpless. They accept the help of government when it steps in, and the advice of doctors, lawyers, and all sorts of experts who tell them what they need.

From politics to economics, from culture to family life, the prodigals have made their wrong turn seem almost the natural way to live. To replace them will not be easy, and may take centuries of concerted effort. But we must recover our social instincts, discard hierarchy, and create a world no longer ruled by power and greed.

The seeds of a new future can already be detected around us. Dissatisfaction with urban life and a longing for a connection with nature are widespread. There is a growing recognition among people that only small communities can be true communities.

In the last 25 years we have seen in America a burgeoning ecological awareness that is in the best sense deeply religious. Coupled with that has been a longing for meaningful work where craft takes priority over mass production. There has already occured a great deal of social experimentation in group living, both in the cities and in the country. With the seeds already planted and beginning to stir, the twenty-first century will be a century of communal family groups.

CHAPTER 2

Laws Promote Crime But Good Mores Can Prevent It

In our society, laws override morality and conscience is replaced by harsh controls. Morality begins in the family group where we are taught compassion and sharing. Law, however, makes us enemies and drives us back to selfish concerns. Each year brings more lawyers and lawsuits, more policemen, and more hours wasted in courts.

The United States now is the home of ten times as many lawyers per capita as Japan, six times as many as Sweden, and far more convicted lawbreakers than anywhere else in the civilized world. We have more juvenile offenders than any other nation, more prisoners per capita, more civil lawsuits. It might fairly be said that America is a society deeply addicted to the law.

Legal reasoning and the legal process have been among the most important foundations of our freedom and among the greatest accomplishments of the human mind. Legal thinkers and law schools have always played a moderating influence in American life—protecting people's rights against the extremist moods of public opinion—and juries have drawn the common person into the discussion of our social problems. But laws are not everything and legislators are pushing them into areas where they do not belong.

Laws tell us only what we cannot do; they do not tell us what we ought to do or how a decent and honest person can be expected to live his life. There are no models of morality for us to copy. There are many things which the law accepts but that conscience tells us are wrong. If we strengthen the family, and spend more time learning in communal family groups, law would not be necessary. People would not need lawyers or judges to tell them what their hearts already know.

It should first of all be pointed out that laws are only really effective by means of the police and the whole criminal justice system of force that is by no means just. The criminal justice system favors the rich, who can afford expensive lawyers with the time and resources to protect their clients. A poor person accused of a crime will be defended by a public defender who is likely to be overworked and underpaid, and who will have incentive to strike a deal with the prosecutor.

So it should be clear that the law as it is applied is unjust. It is also true that the people who commit crimes are often people who have been victimized by serious injustice, hardship and mistreatment of various kinds.

It would only be in a just society that laws could themselves be just, for then no particular group would be more likely than another to commit crimes. But the paradox is that in a truly just society there would be no laws, because there would be no crime. In a society where everyone was already treated fairly no one would feel a need to rob or assault another.

Gerry Spence, a lawyer, points out in his book *With Justice for None*, that there will not be any justice in America because our national purpose is dominated by profit. We are dominated by an amorphous agglomeration of corporations and financial institutions with a passion for money instead of justice. Revenge and the power of forgiveness often wage battles in court but in our alienated and isolated society the winner can usually be foreseen.

Gerry Spence has spent the better part of his life in court protecting the rights of "the little guy" against large corporations. He is in a far better position than most people to assess the business of the criminal justice system.

For starters, Spence points out that people who become lawyers and who are responsible for making the system work, are overwhelmingly white, male, middle or upper-middle class, of European descent. They are eager to become wealthy, highly competitive, and lacking any strong concern for society as a whole.

And of these lawyers, the ones who succeed and eventually become judges are even more wealthy and privileged than their peers. Given a system dominated by such men how can we expect women, minorities or the poor to receive fair treatment? The symbol for justice in America is not the blind woman holding up evenly balanced scales, but the dollar bill.

Nothing illustrates this point better than the case of corporate America as it relates to the law. Spence recounts the story of IBM, one of America's wealthiest corporations. In 1969 the government attempted to prosecute IBM for being in violation of anti-trust laws. Eight years and fifty million dollars later the government threw in the towel on the case.

What happened? IBM assigned hundreds of lawyers to the case from one of the world's top law firms. They had more than three million documents stored in one of the world's largest main frame computers. Another seventeen million were entered in code. IBM had the best lawyers, superior organization and greater resources. There was enormous turnover among the government lawyers. At the end of the case none of the government lawyers who had started out on the case were still prosecuting it.

The government was simply no match for IBM. It takes little reflection to see that it is not justice, but privilege and power that is primarily served in the American criminal justice system. We need to strengthen groups like the communal family and neighborhood that nurture a common morality, and stop depending on laws to hold us together. People who share their lives, developing trust as they seek decisions by consensus in the group, will find that they possess a "sixth sense" about what is right and what is not, what is healthy and what is destructive, and that this goes far deeper than the concepts expressed in laws.

Today all Americans, not just the corporate rich, depend far too greatly on the law. "Sue your neighbor!" is the common cry of insurance attorneys. It has been the good old capitalist way for centuries. Exploit the poor and sue those who are poorer than you.

So addicted are we to law that we have lost the skill and experience of settling things ourselves. We ought to know by now that the best hope for change lies in the love and concern of an integrated communal family group.

As long as American society rests on the dollar as king, with cooperation and shared ownership denigrated, laws, crime and prisons will continue to grow and those least privileged will be the most incarcerated. The solution is to generate humane mores that result in a society where no one feels mistreated and no one feels the need to commit crimes.

CHAPTER 3

Bureaucracy Escapes Responsibility

No doubt many people regard the government as a caretaker, responsible for solving the problems discussed in this book. This, however, is a childish mistake. As government grows larger and more remote by the year, individuals need to do much more, not less, on their own behalf. Rather than complaining to legislators and waiting idly for changes to happen, individuals must form small groups of compatible people to take over the government's tasks. These groups would decide by consensus, the democratic way and the way of our instincts. A large and centralized government, no matter how much it claims to promote the general welfare, always ends up in the hands of the elite.

Government today is so large, so active, so concerned with the minutiae of its citizen's lives that it might well be said we are on the threshold of a new totalitarianism. According to *The Origins of Totalitarianism*, a landmark study by Hannah Arendt, the conditions that gave birth to Stalin and Hitler are not so very different from today. Modern society, according to Arendt, is fragmented into isolated individuals, on the one hand, and impersonal bureaucracies, on the other. The natural communities that nurtured people for thousands of years—family, neighborhood, village, and guild—have either disappeared or are in profound decay. Longing for the trust and cooperativeness that these groups inspire, people feel lonely and helpless and are prepared to let the government step in to satisfy their needs. Even the individual's emotional needs become the objects of state action; nationalism provides a substitute for real community, with its flags, "president worship" and holidays and parades.

In the mass society, as Arendt describes it, even rebels and dissidents are led to make demands on the government when it would be more empowering to try to help themselves. Protests replace action and hierarchies grow up among the protestors themselves. "It is as though mankind had divided itself," she writes, "between those who believe in human omnipotence (who think that everything is possible if one knows how to organize masses for it) and those for whom powerlessness has become the major experience of their lives."

This division is made possible by the invention of bureaucracy. Bureaucracy enables rulers to control a large staff of officials who are interested mostly in their own promotions, and blind either to the needs of individual clients or to the common good they are supposed to serve. Bureaucratic rule helps officials evade responsibility for what they do. Furthermore, bureaucracy presents itself as the only fair and efficient form of government. In doing so, it undermines the confidence of ordinary people who have the potential to live without laws and to rule themselves.

Two other characteristics mark our society as totalitarian in potential, not unlike the Germany of Hitler or Stalin's Soviet Union. The first, according to Arendt, is American imperialism. Imperialism, or the attempt to control other countries, unfailingly strengthens government in its most bureaucratic and hierarchical forms. The attempt to control masses, instead of promoting family group learning, drives individuals apart. Foreign policy always is the most secretive and least democratic branch of politics, the most likely arena for "dirty tricks" and unregulated power. American imperialism has created a network of arms dealers, military programs, spy agencies, defense contractors, and secret funding sources that critics entitle the National Security State. More and more of our scientific economy is secretly funded by the government for military use, and material that is classified grows apace.

Bureaucracy Escapes Responsibility

The second force that pulls us toward totalitarianism is the mounting power of corporations and their merger with the state. It is widely known that a tiny percentage of Americans hold half our corporate stock. Perhaps less widely known is that an even smaller fraction make the important decisions within the "Fortune 1000," and by doing so, control the movement of resources and manpower across the face of the earth.

Economic power translates into political control. Large corporations are the source for more campaign funds than all other groups and individuals combined. Nearly every Senator, along with many Congressmen, own substantial amounts of corporate stock. Both political parties, no matter what their rhetoric, find themselves forced to cater to corporate needs.

What is worse, the Bill of Rights is left outside the corporate door. Employees in American society have scarcely more right to criticize corporate policy than did employees in Nazi Germany, let alone the right to decide such policies for themselves. This has resulted in a society of apathetic people, who justify their actions with the claim that they are "just following orders."

Perhaps the darkest example of corporate power, and one that is rarely discussed, is the rapidly growing concentration of media ownership across the earth. In many nations, these monopolies that control information and entertainment are sparking public outcry. But in the United States three or four mammoth chains dominate the media without causing a whimper. Active in newspapers, television networks, movie and video production, and cable TV, the media monopolies are intertwined in ownership with electronics firms and leading contractors of the Pentagon. It is not likely they will criticize the government, and even less likely that they will criticize themselves.

There are many things we can do to reverse the drift toward totalitarianism. Most of all, we can recover the communal family group, where humankind learned over the course of millenia to develop trust, confidence, and cooperative skills. We must place less faith in big organizations and their laws, and more faith in our own human powers. We must work locally, building communities that not only protest but serve concrete needs. By caring for our land, our tools, and our children in common, we will come to strengthen the social skills and self-respect needed for other tasks of self-government, including the development of meaningful work, the protection of societies weaker than our own, and the conservation of the earth. Togetherness, empathy and sharing are more important than sexuality, procreation or the power of numbers.

CHAPTER 4

Religion Free of Hierarchy

Human beings today are strangers to their ancestors and traditions, to their neighborhoods and communities, and above all they are estranged from the land. This frightful isolation is rooted in the biases of the Judeo-Christian religion and will destroy the planet itself if we do not change it. Such is the passsionate warning of Vine Deloria, Native American philosopher and activist, who implores Americans to learn from Indian cultures before it is too late.

Most Americans, Deloria writes, have never been at home in this land. This is not only because most of us are immigrants or descendants of immigrants who have continued to wander over the face of the continent, but also because most of the founding fathers were believers in a "sky god", who taught that the earth was only a temporary abode. For the followers of the Christian God, the earth and its wonders was simply the location of the long upward climb, the "Pilgrim's Progress," which was to end gloriously in heaven.

The sky religion emphasizes hierarchy, self-denial, and endless striving to perfect oneself in the eyes of a demanding God. Over the centuries, particularly since the Protestant Reformation, it has produced lonely individualists, who are restless, competitive, and in a profound sense "homeless" both in space and in time. The terrible irony is that the great new home for the homeless, America, the leading Protestant nation, was itself based on a massive theft of homeland (of the Indians) and a forcible uprooting from home (of Negro Slaves).

Sickened by all this, many Americans, especially the young, have for the past three decades been exploring a sharply different religious tradition. Older than the sky religions, it is what Deloria has called the Earth Culture and it celebrates nature as a "mother". Long ago the American Indians (and other tribal peoples) found what we in our discontent still are seeking. They were at home in their land, in the cosmos, and in their bodies. Unlike the sky religion, the earth tradition emphasizes the maternal, communal, and joyful aspects of existence. Where the sky religions see fathers, teachers, rulers, and gods exercising external control through laws or force, the earth tradition is attuned to cosmic harmonies and interpersonal influence. Socially the Earth Culture expresses itself not though impersonal bureaucracy or the isolated nuclear family, but through communes, tribes, and large extended families. In its rituals, the earth religion is like an elaborate dance giving expression to all the forces of the universe and to the role of each person in his society.

Land plays a singular role in the earth religion. It is not in church, but in the sacred mountains and rivers and on the tribal burial grounds that Native Americans can be in contact with the spiritual powers that have always guided the tribe. In many cases the land itself is given a voice on the tribal council. Nurturance of the land is as important to the religious communities as are healing ceremonies for the individual.

In America, the existence of intact Indian cultures like the Pueblo and the Navaho is an incomparable treasure. This battered remnant of a decimated people, gaining voice at last through its leaders, may yet provide the saving wisdom that will make possible our renewal.

A familiar picture exists of religious life in America which encourages us to believe that religion is primarily a force that brings people together and makes them feel like they belong to a close knit community. While there is some truth to this notion it masks a deeper, more important truth.

It is true many people today believe themselves religious and to have empathy and compassion by their habit of tithing 10 percent, or even 15 percent, of their income. This leaves them free to follow their capitalist urge to buy cheap and sell dear, or make trades that are essentially unfair. This kind of life is common in America today but can be changed when people learn to share what they have with others and to integrate their lives with people less fortunate.

Few things isolate people as much as ignorance and fear. These make one a prisoner of his own narrow group and are a powerful force for conformity. On the other hand nothing strengthens the soul so much as imagination, curiosity, and the passion to share what one has learned.

Learning liberates the spirit when it awakens and rewards the student's own powers to explore and understand reality. Nowhere is this liberation conveyed with more drama and delight than in the story of Helen Keller, the books of neurologist Oliver Sacks, or in Susan Schaller's tale of her long and arduous effort to make contact with a 27 year-old "languageless" man. All of these works tremble with the excitement felt by disabled people emerging from deep ignorance, aided for the most part only by sheer desire to learn. They urge us to appreciate the astonishing changes wrought in people once deprived of understanding, but now introduced by loving teachers to a world of numbers and words. More than anything, it is the sheer thirst and hunger of the mind that is the true subject of these outspoken books. It is the mind's passion to make sense of the world, and to reach out to minds like itself, that explains the miraculous progress of a Helen Keller or the deaf "man without words" called Ildefonso. Perhaps this passion is cherished by the self-educated more than by those who have spent their lives in school. In any event, the mind's instinctual hunger to understand is surely the most powerful force in nature. It is a force that our spiritual training must nurture and guide, not humiliate and repress.

Religious hierarchy squelches our inborn curiosity. It is a terrible fact that human beings, whose brains are far larger than the chimpanzee's, use a much smaller portion of their brains and permit most members of their species to languish in ignorance. Religion accepts this tragic reality, even encourages it, for ignorance is associated with hierarchy and Western religion is one of the most hierarchical social orders on earth.

It is hardly surprising that a religion which invented God the patriarch, surrounded Him with a priestly elite, and built a wealthy and bureaucratic Church by taxing the labor of the masses, would frown on all efforts to abolish hierarchy and extend education and enlightenment to everyone. Ever since Abraham made his covenant with God, the Judeo-Christian religion has stressed the contrast between the Lord's perfection and humankind's sin, between the mysterious grandeur of God's creation and man's puny mind. No other civilization, not even the Greeks, established so great a distance between God and man nor so steep a hierarchy among men themselves. Even the churches today do not really value cooperation and consensus. In the Catholic Church there are the bishops and priests; but among the Protestants too there is management by professionals and the biggest donors retain the greatest say.

The dollar bill of the United States provides one vivid example of the religious belief in monarchy and the hierarchy of God. It indicates distrust of the common man as it was expressed by our founding fathers and framers of the constitution. The statement on bills and coins which says "In God We Trust" implies that we don't trust people. And the statement "Legal tender for all debts public and private" suggests that we are responsible for the public debts of irresponsible representatives.

It is important to see how much God has been used to justify hierarchy. Since God is male, men must be superior to women, and since God towers over all of humanity, it is legitimate for a few human beings to lord over the masses.

Power as it exists in the world cannot be separated from religion. It is time that we finally stop seeing religion as a fortress of moral purity and begin to admit to ourselves that religion is an ally of political power. It is no less a political evil than laws or government.

Religious hierarchy is opposed to human evolution and to human equality, notwithstanding the fact that for the past two centuries equality has been on the rise. Nowadays a chosen few live without hierarchy—mostly academics, artists, and scientists. Yet our religious and cultural training keep us from seeing that the academic paradise of lifelong learning and freedom could be extended to all. With education to dispel our ignorance, we could all fulfill our brain's potential and live freely, outside the hierarchies of corporation, bureaucracy, and school.

The oneness of life in communal families can restore us to the wisdom of our instincts and to the proper use of our entire brains. When this happens hierarchies will automatically disappear and take their rightful place in the ash heap of history. What is a liberating religion? This is a difficult question, but one which the remainder of this chapter will endeavor to answer. Religion, properly understood, should be something that evokes a feeling of awe and reverence towards the universe, and towards ourselves as a manifestation of nature. It ought to be a force that brings us together, not in shared delusions about reality, but by helping us see that we are ultimately part of a larger whole.

What religion should be is something that deepens our appreciation of, and connection to nature. It should also represent a call to people to gather in groups and seek a deeper understanding and expression of their emotions as they stand in nature's beauty and splendor.

The world, it is clear, is heading toward disaster. With the population rapidly increasing, more and more people are living squalid lives that end in premature, needlessly painful deaths. As overpopulation burdens humanity, nature too is being quickly destroyed, and with it the capacity of humans to relate deeply to nature. It is possible that within a century or two there will be no one left who has communed with nature in solitude. Fewer and fewer people have had the experience of being close to animals in the wild or really appreciating the rhythms of nature. When humans lose touch with this experience they are in danger of losing their concrete grasp of the interconnectedness of all things.

Fortunately, there still exist adventurous souls who have gone off into nature and recounted their experiences. Such a person is Michael Modzelewski, a free-spirited man who spent a year and a half living on a desolate island in the Inside Passage, a couple of hundred miles north of Vancouver, Canada. Modzelewski describes his experiences in his book *Inside Passage*.

It is difficult to say simply what he discovered during his eighteen months away from the civilization he'd grown up in. He had intimate experiences with animals, with the landscape, and with the Kwakiutl Indians which altered his sense of who he was, and made him feel at home in the universe. Although he had far less human contact than he was accustomed to, he discovered that he felt less lonely than he had in the past. Modzelewski felt a spiritual kinship with all creatures. He began to feel at home in the world in a way he never had before. He felt in his bones the truth that he and nature were the same.

Modzelewski understood that the attempt by modern man to treat nature as something to be conquered was a disastrous mistake that grew out of feelings of isolation and alienation. He describes an experience in a boat trying to catch fish. He saw a school of herring in the water being chased by a school of salmon from below. Above the water sea gulls swooped down and ate the fish that were leaping out of the sea. Seals and sea lions also appeared to eat their fill. Then, off in the distance, he saw some killer whales.

Modzelewski decided to get into the act. He hit the water with his oar and scooped up half a dozen herring, which he soon ate. As he did this he had a revelation. He understood for the first time that the food chain was not an abstract idea, but that he himself was integrally connected to it. He saw that no matter how far humans try to rise above the animal world they will always be a part of the cycles of nature.

As humans despoil nature there exist fewer and fewer opportunities to experience first hand what Modzelewski experienced. It is not enough to simply read or think in the abstract about connections to nature. It must be deeply felt. This can only happen when people relate to nature first hand. Communing with nature, as he did, is the true religious experience. Religious worship ought to be a celebration of the connection between people, calling on us to overcome isolation, separation, and hierarchy.

The first religions saw the sacred as manifest in the wind and the rain and the sun and moon. God was nature. God was all around man and inseparable from nature. The connection that humans felt with nature created a feeling of shared wonder which bonded people together and made them feel at one. Religion should evoke experience of shared wonder to bring people together. We need to dispense with all talk about God and instead speak of the sacred.

Zen Buddhism provides another concrete example of a religion with liberating force. The Zen Buddhist masters see the Buddha nature in everyone and treat each person with compassion. To become a better person, one becomes a vehicle by which others find their own nature. This is similar to the Quaker belief that there is an inner light in every man and each person's duty is to help others discover it. Such a belief causes every Quaker to become a social worker.

David Brandon in his book, *Zen in the Art of Helping,* describes his experiences as a Buddhist and a social worker where he became preoccupied with the problem of homelessness. The men and women he worked with had been divested of almost everything—family, social relations, adequate clothing and money, proper food and shelter. He spent years talking to people who lived in derelict houses, under rail bridges and in parks. Little stuck to them. They were concerned with the present moment—the next meal, the next handout, the next bed. He says, "It is no accident that so many religious leaders chose to be drifters and to live without a settled home. Having a home can result in a narrowing of vision; having too comfortable an armchair to travel anywhere in. Religious leaders have to float ideologically to challenge prevailing views of life. Every day the homeless man looks for shelter from the wind and rain. Everyday he is sensitive to changes in the weather, to the different seasons. Life blows him about like an autumn leaf. The cost of his shelterlessness brings bronchitis, frostbite or TB often from alcoholism and crawling fleas. He becomes an object of social charity to be shaped by their services. He is defined as a beggar, a street person. His sense of humanity is eroded."

Religion Free of Hierarchy

Brandon celebrates the virtues of constructive restlessness. To grow in mind and body is to live iconoclastically. It is necessary to have neither too much nor too little. The poor are eternally preoccupied with pangs of hunger and sodden with rain; the wealthy spend their time acquiring and protecting what they have. Only a man not imprisoned by the weight of his possessions and yet not obsessed with the need to find food and shelter can ask and live out important questions; Who am I? Where am I going? What is the nature of life? These answers can be found by creating and living in communal family groups which follow our human instincts.

CHAPTER 5

From Medical Malaise to Free Group Healthcare

Modern medicine is impressive, with its advanced technology and scientific research. But the critics are right who say that its miracles are exaggerated and the medical establishment cannot see the forest for the trees.

Many doctors fail to see that the medical problems a person suffers from may be the result of a broad combination of unhealthy forces operating in our society. As social critic Ivan Ilych has shown, improved sanitation and better health education make more difference than technology. Advertising exploits people's health for profit and often makes money more important than an individual's health or welfare. Doctors are treating symptoms rather than the causes.

People in physical distress most often want their doctor to give them a quick fix to remove the discomfort and get them back to their busy lives. Most Americans are too busy chasing the dollar to slow down and give serious attention to their health. The traditional way of medicine is still very common. Someone who is suffering from a headache goes to a doctor and after establishing that no serious illness is causing the headache, the doctor prescribes two aspirin. If the headache doesn't go away he will prescribe a stronger painkiller.

The doctor's role ought to be changed. It should be to educate the patient about things he can do to improve his health. The problem is that doctors themselves are only beginning to acknowledge the multitude of things that influence health.

A long-term study of 7,000 people conducted by "Prevention," a health magazine, found that simple nutrition and exercise are better for our health than fancy medical techniques. Today many educated people are taking a more enlightened, holistic approach to their health. They eat a balanced diet, high in fruits, vegetables, and grains, and low in cholestrol and fat; they swim, run, or engage in some other aerobic exercise; and they do not smoke or drink. The better educated are also more enlightened about the nature of mental health.

The real job of doctors ought to be to make themselves unnecessary and superfluous. It is ironic that while everyone knows "an ounce of prevention is worth a pound of cure," so few people actually practice it. It is estimated that roughly a third of all cancers could be eliminated if people simply quit smoking.

Were people to live in rural villages and be housed in communal family groups, exercise and fresh air would add to their health. With fresh fruits and vegetables their nutrition would be immensely improved. Plucking an apple right off the tree, or an ear of corn straight from the stalk, children would find eating delightful, and soon forget about the fast food joints or the "Seven Eleven." Since farming, gardening, and construction would be part of every person's experience, exercise would become woven fully into the fabric of life. And since meaningful work and joyful relationships would be available to all, people would rely less on drinking or smoking, or invisible crutches like prescription pills and TV.

PSYCHOTHERAPY

Psychotherapy has become one of the commonest ways Americans cope with their problems and one of the largest growth industries in the U.S. It is useful to people going through difficult periods in their lives. But in fundamental ways, therapy is flawed. Its basic weakness is that, like medicine, it treats the symptoms and not the causes of people's suffering. The message is clear; it is the patient who must change his life. In one sense this is quite reasonable. After all, the therapist can't be expected to change the world. It is much easier to adjust the client to difficult living conditions than it is to change those conditions.

All too often a person's problems are not his alone. Rather they are created by the failure of his society to offer him certain things that everyone needs, like meaningful work and the possibility of intimacy with both men and women. In therapy as in medicine, people have begun to take responsibility for their mental health, often by forming groups.

CHAPTER 6

Media, That Insidious Goliath

The media is an enormous subject and one that has become so big it is almost impossible to calculate its complex and subtle influence on our lives. It is really difficult to know, for example, how our minds and our thinking would be different if we had never watched television or listened to the radio. Advertising by TV and the press does the opposite of what education does. As a person learns, education broadens one's understanding and acceptance of differences in ethnic backgrounds, skin color, or the physical and mental problems of poverty others suffer from. There are far more people in the world who live in ghettos than live in affluence. Most of us know very little of the intimate lives of those who are different from us.

Advertising works by creating what are called wants. Wants are easily distinguished from true human needs. True human needs are such things as love, intimacy, community, learning, meaningful creative work, ownership of a living space, and closeness to nature. If all these needs are met, a person is affluent in the true sense and false wants cannot easily be created by advertising. It is only in a society where people are not getting what they truly need and have lost touch with themselves that they will be so concerned with whether their car has a fancy new fin, or if their shirt has the latest style collar.

What is most characteristic of wants is that they're never really satisfied. Consumerism works by providing people with things that leave them momentarily stimulated but ultimately unfulfilled. It's like eating junk food, full of sugar and spices and fats, but lacking in nutrition. Advertising makes us feel inadequate if we don't possess whatever is being advertised.

Advertising functions in a way almost exactly opposite of how psychotherapy is supposed to function. Psychotherapy is designed to examine our dreams and fantasies and thoughts to help us understand what we really feel so we may understand our past behavior and act with clarity and appropriateness in the future. Therapy, ideally at least, is meant to make us feel whole.

Advertising fragments us by exploiting feelings and desires we are only partially aware of. After a therapy session we are supposed to have a better sense of who we are. After being exposed to advertising we are less in touch with ourselves.

Television and radio in particular have become companions for many people. Like all companions they provide distraction from feelings of loneliness and boredom. By offering easy stimulation and momentary pleasure, television in particular satisfies wants and enables people to ignore their true needs.

It's a common scene that all Americans are familiar with: a family sits together in the living room, staring hypnotically at the television set. If anyone speaks, the rest of the family shuts them up. It is as if everyone has gone into a trance that enables them to avoid intimacy with each other. What matters is not so much the content of television but the way it allows people to avoid each other. As has often been remarked, it is like a drug, a psychic painkiller.

Parents, it is claimed, do not spend enough "quality time" with their kids. It is almost a form of child abuse the way some parents get their kids to watch television so that they will remain quiet and stay occupied. They are often shocked to learn that their children are taking drugs or having sex or otherwise breaking the law.

Television also serves to compensate people for the drudgery and lack of excitement they suffer in their everyday lives. The high-school student who on her teacher's orders must memorize a pile of meaningless facts, or a file clerk trapped in his monotonous job, can through television's magic prowl the streets of Al Capone's Chicago or the foggy alleys of Victorian London. The outrageous level of violence on television can be explained in this way. Violence, of course, is exciting. But it also allows people to express the aggression that they feel during long hours serving the boss or the demands of a machine. Television helps to distract people from the problems of the social order and keeps them from taking steps to transform their lives.

Many TV shows, like the crime programs or "horror" films, wrap their violence in an atmosphere that can only be called psychotic. Paranoia, cruelty, and obsessive sex pervade these shows; and it is hard to say what is worse, when the viewer identifies with their villain or when he identifies with the victim. But on television, abnormality is presented as normal and brutality is made to seem almost glamorous. Perhaps half of all prime-time dramas constitute an invitation to participate in insanity and pathological thinking.

There are three areas of life where TV is destroying people's lives and especially those of Americans. One is that it is creating for us an artificial environment where we have lost contact with our planet. We are becoming disconnected and floating in space like the astronauts. We don't know up from down or truth from fiction.

Second, TV is dominated by a handful of corporations, which are using it to create a new form of human being. This new human type is passive, impulsive, and submissive to the multinational powers or totalitarianism that is gaining control of our lives. He is an individualist, a competitor, and a consumer, like the prodigals of the corporate world who brought him to life. It is a conspiracy of economic and technological factors that make this almost inevitable.

Third, the technology of television produces physiological responses in people who watch it. It may create illness and it certainly produces confusion and submission to external imagery. Taken together the effects amount to conditioning for automatic control.

Perhaps as great a threat as television is the current fascination with computers. Computers are in danger of destroying society. Everything that is bad about bureaucracies can be made worse by computers. The dangerous centralization of power that has occurred in the modern state has dramatically increased with the advent of computers. We have only begun to see the potential for bureaucratic control by the state that computers can unleash.

Our growing dependency on computers is frightening. How many times have we heard people say, "The computer is down"? Organizations go into a state of helpless chaos without computers. How many times do our bank deposits not go through because of a computer foul up?

And how often is our privacy invaded because someone has gotten our name and address and telephone number from a computer? Junk mail and telephone calls are a growing problem. We are also using computers to raise our children, at home and in the schools. When both parents are employed, it is tempting to rely on the lifelike excitement of the computer game or teaching machine, as a kind of babysitter. Many children grow up as a result with less human contact than they really need.

The growing reliance on computers exemplifies a major problem with technology. People believe that if they can use new technology to do something then they should use that technology. Computers make a good servant but a poor master. Like so much modern technology, they have become an end in themselves. So many people believe that if they can put something on a computer, then they should. Computers give people a false sense of control. As life gets more hectic and people feel their lives going out of control, computers offer a distracting and illusory feeling of power. They offer a poor substitute for the community and sense of purpose that humans really need.

No study of the media would be complete without some words about the press. The U.S. has an impressive array of print media, 1700 daily newspapers and 11,000 magazines. Unfortunately, however, as media watchdog Ben Bagdikian has shown, most of these sources are owned by the same two or three dozen corporations, who seldom refrain from using their power to promote corporate values. The chief officers of the twenty corporations that control most of what Americans read can fit into an ordinary living room. Almost without exception they are conservative Republicans. Bagdikian documents numerous occasions on which they have used their monopoly to stifle dissenting voices and push the values of the marketplace. The parent firms of most of the major media are part of the corporate power that has squeezed the life out of our local communities and their libraries and museums. Bagdikian proposes a number of media reforms. But beyond these, we need something far bolder like the recovery of vital communal life. People who feel involved in their communal groups do not need to be passively entertained. They are less bewitched by advertising and more enlightened and critical about the news. They have a wider frame of social experience against which they can measure and evaluate what they read.

At times it seems that one of the dying arts of the twentieth century is the art of self entertainment. For thousands of years people lived without movies, without television, without tourism, without having money to spend in a vast consumer marketplace. The progress of technology has made life in some ways easier and more comfortable, but our habitual reliance upon it has alienated us from one of our most precious possessions: our capacity to give ourselves joy using our own talents. Consider a group of people singing together; a kind of fusion develops in which everyone for a short while is feeling the same thing. This can happen when music is a non-competitive expression of common feelings. In the world of communal family living people will relearn the art of having fun. Entertainment will be valued as a form of activity.

Some questions that must be asked about any particular form of entertainment are: Does it make people feel more or less isolated? In other words, after having engaged in it do people feel closer to each other or further apart? And does it challenge their creative abilities or simply reinforce their passivity?

Intimacy is a concept that is far more complex than we often think. Most people think of intimacy in terms of two people revealing their innermost thoughts and feelings.

There is another kind of intimacy that has to do with group enjoyment. I refer to what might be called the intimacy of good times shared together. When people in a group engage in a fun activity that hurts no one, psychologically or physically, they are not being intimate in the sense of sharing private feelings.

But they are being intimate in another sense; they are sharing themselves and their good will.

In any group entertainment, competition is an issue that must be dealt with. In some activities—virtually in any games, whether they require physical skill or mental astuteness—competition is necessary. Someone has to do better, and someone has to do worse. It is a challenge to find ways to make competition enjoyable and non-alienating. The trick is to learn the right attitude towards competition, one in which people enjoy the challenge of playing a game well, but have no need to feel triumphant or to make someone else feel humiliated. Entertainment that is active, challenging, often skillful, and that bridges the distances between people is what we need to counter the insidious spread of mass media, especially TV.

CHAPTER 7

George Washington: America was Founded on Prodigality

The territory covered by the present United States of America was not always privately owned by the white man. Until about 1000 A.D. when Viking explorers claimed these shores for their king, America was owned by nobody, not even its natives themselves. The native inhabitants lived as guests on the land. They lacked even the concept of an owner, lord, or master.

As the Europeans arrived, pushing inland on their hunt for gold, silver and Indian slaves, everything began to rapidly change. Merchants made fortunes building ships and marketing furs, cutting down the forests and killing wildlife as if Creation had been dreamed up just for their selfish wants. Waves of settlement brought farmers, who razed the wilderness and dumped refuse into the rivers and lakes.

But the worst exploitation in early America was carried out on the backs of servants and slaves, on the plantations of the tobacco-growing South. And in this world of the landed rich, none were harder or more money-minded than the Washingtons of Virginia. Ridding the land of Indians, they planted tobacco on thousands of fertile acres granted through political connections that tied them to the English king. Most Americans would probably be appalled if they knew that George Washington, the father of their country, owned more slaves, more servants, and more inherited land than all but a handful of his countrymen.

Who was George Washington? At the time of his inauguration in 1790, the founding father of American "democracy" owned 35,000 prime acres in Virginia and 1100 in Maryland, including water rights on several rivers. He owned several thousand head of livestock, numerous small factories and farms, and many hundreds of slaves. In addition Washington owned lucrative properties in two American cities and two British towns. He owned shares in three private companies, and as the holder of sizable public bonds, stood to profit from the workings of the United States government itself. Today Washington would be a multimillionaire or perhaps a trillionaire.

But of course George Washington was more than just another wealthy landowner. He was "the father of his country." He was, according to the legend, a statesman, in possession of a vision that pierced beyond his own selfish interests to include the common good of his colony of Virginia, and later, of the entire nation. Yet even the vision was myopic. Washington's vision for the country was the deeply biased outlook of a prodigal—a man who has learned from the cradle to exploit nature's plenty for his own selfish purposes.

While in office, for example, Washington threw his support behind the new constitution, which centralized power in the federal government and the executive branch and deprived common people of many rights they had enjoyed within their states.

We have been misguided in our admiration for George Washington. His popularity as the Father of our country reflects our need to remain helpless children, unable to take responsibility for our lives. We must give up the need for mythic heroes and look for concrete ways to improve our lives and those of our neighbors.

CHAPTER 8

New Relations Between the Genders

Today we need less sex, fewer births, and more recognition of what both females and males can contribute to the human family. We need to move beyond the nuclear family, which emphasizes sex and procreation, and create communal families where there is sharing and friendship between men and women. Eventually we may abolish gender differences altogether.

For centuries the nuclear family served humanity by raising the birth rate, though women and children were heavily exploited. Many rulers relied on it to supply workers and soldiers to the state. But today our population is exploding and threatens to sweep humanity and every other species toward armageddon. In Haiti, Mexico, or Bangladesh, families with 15 children are not uncommon, and population growth fuels endless political turmoil. We must begin to put love and friendship in the place of procreative sex.

The nuclear family is obsolete for a second reason as well. It intensifies the differences between men and women, and isolates the couple from the outside world. Today we are dangerously overspecialized: women depend on men economically, and men depend on women to express emotions and protect the softer side of life. Just like the worker who can do only one job and finds himself at the mercy of his employer, so do couples find themselves locked into a marriage which is merely economic. In this situation sex often becomes a weapon and a source of great confusion.

If we were to live in communal family groups of 15 to 20 people, relationships would be far more relaxed. Like the children of the kibbutz, boys and girls would grow up side by side, sharing life together in a spirit of friendship. Each person would learn a far greater range of skills and emotional expression, so that nobody would seek a mate for economic reasons or to feel complete. Each person would also have more companions and a firmer sense of place in the community.

We all know how complex and surprising our partners become when we interact with them as part of a group, at a party or some social event. We perceive them anew. Qualities we might never have dreamed of are drawn out of them by others. Even more enlivening is when partners share some project that makes a difference in the world. Men and women need to experience one another beyond the bedroom and the dinner table, to engage themselves in the kind of shared moral vision that can be experienced in a communal family.

Neither sex nor marriage will be a substitute for friendship or community or the need to create meaning in one's life. Sexual differences will then take their rightful place as part of life's fulfillment.

Sexual diversity would be celebrated rather than condemned in a communal family group. Gays and lesbians would be accepted as whole human beings. People who want lots more sex would be free to seek it and those who want less can avoid it; neither type would feel the guilt they are now made to feel. The stigma that so often attaches to anyone who is a little different would be gone.

The state should withdraw from the bedroom. The government should not be telling us how to run the intimate details of our lives. The state can be replaced by the family spirit of acceptance.

Marriage controlled by the state fixes the loyalties of the couple on one another and isolates them from the group. It creates a kind of private property in affections that only worsens when children appear on the scene, because children are owned by their parents as women are owned by men. The narcissism of the couple, not sexuality, was the force that distracted human beings from the larger group and its spiritual ideals. Sexual freedom in the climate of a group intimately responsible for life is not sexual license nor sexual abandonment. Such models for children create trust in life and adult behavior. The most important result of these sexual changes will be to slow the birth rate and begin to stem the over population that threatens our survival on this planet. Experts who debate the reasons for this explosion of births often overlook a significant source. Many people today bear children neither out of material self-interest nor in obedience to their religion, but because they hunger to be admired and loved. Sex and procreation alike give them an escape from anonymity, a feeling that they are valuable and necessary.

A second reason for over-population is that in a society based on nuclear families, rather than on instinct, women have lost their power to limit family size. In every species, females are the caretakers of the group. They nurture the young and care for the sick and the elderly; they embody the forces of love and cooperation, and they tend to heal the wounds caused by conflict. Females also strengthen the group in a subtler and less visible way; they control the birth rate by instigating conception only when new babies are needed.

Thus women have the instinctual power to curb population growth. But their oppression by lustful males, prodigals, has kept them from expressing their instincts for over 5000 years. The harmony of our instincts has been sacrificed to shortsighted greed. Only in communal family groups, where women share power and each adult depends on every other, will our terrifying birth rates finally be reduced.

The evidence suggests that human fertility rose sharply with the advent of agriculture around 4000 B.C., and again at the time of the Industrial Revolution. What is interesting about these jumps in births is that both coincided with the rise in state power and the decline of communal family groups. Both were creations of the prodigals. While the relationships between these changes must have been complex, it is hard to resist the conclusion that without communal groups to depend on, prodigals propagated children as a way of increasing their own power. Just as prodigals desired a growing population of subjects, so adults came to rely on the services of their children, once they could not depend on help from one another.

This pattern which survives in most of the world has become a time bomb imperiling our survival. Human beings have become bereft of all power and affection except what they can command from their offspring. The prodigals' exploitation of women for their wombs, along with their repression of women's brains, has been suicidial both for the human race and planet earth. We must move beyond gender and invite men and women to share their affections in a spirit of closeness and friendship.

CHAPTER 9

Stimulating the Brain Increases Its Potential

Recent studies have shown that boredom is one important cause of the mental ailments that plague us in the modern world. Boredom reflects a lack of ingenuity about the world which has its roots both in the structure of the family and the failure of the educational system. Our bureaucratic society regards emotions as disruptive and dangerous, and allows little room for their expression. But when emotions are repressed, all sorts of illness will arise.

Students of animal behavior widely agree that emotional expression has been vital to the evolution of humans. Intelligent mammals such as pigs and chimpanzees show a wide repertoire of feelings ranging from excitement and joy, to anger, anxiety, and fear. Strong feelings help to motivate animals as they explore their world, and thus assist the development of learning. Repressing feelings, on the other hand, leads not only to boredom but to the atrophy of our mental powers.

Nowhere is the problem more severe than in the poor nations of the third world. Here, apathy and passivity are due not only to society's emphasis on routine but also to unemployment, ignorance, and want. Colonialism robbed native peoples of more than their natural resources; it deprived them of initiative, responsibility and stimulating work. In many countries, as in the ghettoes of the United States, there is an obvious decline of willpower and creative thought, which has measurable effects on the brain itself. Shocking as it may sound, throughout the world we are day by day making ourselves stupid.

The atrophy of our brains can be reversed, by providing both better nutrition and a more stimulating environment. We can increase stimulation by the social relationships we create and the challenges we arrange for ourselves. Of course the smarter we become, the more stimulation and excitement we will be able to dream up.

The basic point is a simple one. A variety of studies of mammals, especially rats, indicate that an enriched, more stimulating environment can literally improve brain size. This is spelled out by Marion Diamond in her book *Enriching Heredity*. Access to stimulating, challenging objects, Diamond points out, produces a thicker cerebral cortex and larger neurons, both of which are key factors in problem solving. The other side of the point is equally important. Environments that do not provide stimulation and challenge inhibit the growth of the brain and can reduce the size and number of cells.

It is important to see that these findings apply to mammals of all ages. It appears that all human beings can improve the functioning of their brains by altering the environment they live in, no matter what their age. At every age where environmental effects were studied, anatomical changes were noticed in the brain.

Most of this research was done with rats who were placed in either enriched or impoverished environments. An impoverished environment was one where the rat lived alone in a small bare cage, whereas an enriched one consisted of a very large cage with twelve rats and all kinds of toys and nooks and crannies. What was clear from the cumulative research is that rats who lived in enriched environments were more intelligent and possessed better developed brains than the other rats. In one study that involved elderly rats, the animals actually lined up in front of their cage to see what challenging new toys would be introduced for the day.

Stimulating the Brain Increases Its Potential

In other studies, scientists increased the lifespan of mammals, not only by providing them with new mental challenges, but even more by showing them extra love and attention. Rats with deprived brains—whether the offspring of protein-deprived mothers, or victims of brain damage in infancy—were almost wholly rehabilitated when placed in an enriched environment. With proper stimulation, even very old animals enlarged their brains to as great a degree as the young.

Of course we cannot directly apply findings from work performed on rats to human beings. Nevertheless, the basic principles are the same. Most of what scientists have learned about the human nervous system and its growth has been the result of studies on rats and other mammals.

Discoveries like these are exciting, but shouldn't really surprise us. We all know that some environments excite us while others are depressing. The issue is certainly more complex for humans, but the challenge remains very clear; we must create enriched living spaces that will make us more vital and intelligent human beings.

Specifically, stimulating our brains means that our educational system must be radically transformed. We search frantically for new sources of wealth and energy, forgetting that by far the greatest source of untapped energy lies in our young people.

The current approach to education is misguided. The goal of education must not be to produce people who can fit into a technocratic society and find a technical skill they can sell in a job market. By shifting the whole educational system to the care of villages and communal family groups, every person will receive free a high quality life-long education extending to PhD programs and beyond. For shared lives no expense or care will be too great. There will be fewer failed students, disgruntled teachers, or drop outs. As the waste of the prodigals is converted to the development of human instincts, education will be inseparable from living itself.

CHAPTER 10

Invest in the Future, Invest in People

One thing must occur if we are to make the transformation from a highly competitive society to a cooperative one. We must provide an incentive for people to invest their time and money in communal family businesses. These businesses will be collectively owned and efficiently run and will produce larger dividends and more wealth than is possible with any stock corporation. And their results will be far more long-lasting. As a result communal families will be well stocked with capital and will not need to borrow.

Work in a communal family group will differ so much from what we now know as work that we will need a completely new word for it. Communal businesses combine the love and trust of family life with the social responsibility and sense of purpose that are found in a few enlightened enterprises. It is important to try to imagine how these businesses will work.

Today's family farm, though it is only one step in the right direction, provides some clues as to how communal business will prosper. Obviously, many family farms have been narrow-minded and tyrannical. But at their best, family farms have been able to match and even exceed the accomplishments of big agribusiness—and without its exploitation, health hazards, and reliance on government hand-outs. Family members take on the jobs which suit them and work at a pace that fits their needs. Everyone sees the importance of what they do and knows something about the jobs of others. Work is simply another way for people to get to know one another. If there is a single theme I have hammered home, it is the importance of self reliance and reliance upon small communal family groups. This of course means ceasing to rely on governments, but it also means ceasing to rely on experts and being willing to place trust in one's own experience.

Wendell Berry, in addition to being one of America's finest writers, is a farmer. He has travelled all over the world studying different kinds of agriculture, often in an attempt to learn age-old techniques of indigenous peoples who are threatened by the advent of new technology. Berry believes that the modern advent of agribusiness is destructive to the land, the quality of our food, and to the culture itself.

He describes an international week long conference on hill agriculture held in West Virginia, with several state and federal agencies and a private foundation in attendance. There were many academic and government experts delivering papers on the problems of growing food on hills. The papers were very specialized and technical and not a soul there could give a general overview of the problem.

But what was most striking to Berry was the absence of farmers!

Farmers were absent in part because many could not afford to be there or were too busy farming to talk about farming. But they were also absent because they were not being thought about.

Experts were giving papers on agricultural technology and technique without considering the economic, political, or cultural effects on farmers. It occurred to Berry that rather than solving problems, the experts were themselves a problem! The problem they exemplified was how to get the experts and bureaucracies to understand the lives of everyday workers, in this case farmers, in such a way that their expertise is useful. How are we to get the experts to understand that they have as much to learn from farmers as they have to teach? So many experts are lost in abstractions and research that their ideas are useless. Experts have to learn to talk with people and not just to them.

We need the technical expertise that such people have to offer, but we need to learn to apply it concretely in our work and lives. And we need to understand that all workers have something to contribute.

In the communal family shop or factory, these advantages are taken even further. Employees work with their relatives and friends. They make their decisions collectively—ideally, by consensus. Business is a part of family life, and it is the family that decides when and how the work will be performed.

In a communal factory, for example, the group divides its jobs flexibly, so that everyone can learn interesting things, move around the site, and meet new people. Employees as owners will develop social relationships beyond the wildest dreams of today's narrowly-trained "wage-slaves." Imagine building a table with your neighbors one week and the next week designing an innovative lamp with your housemates! Or inventing a new kind of paint and marketing it yourself, then using the profits to start something entirely new. In any communal business, people will share their ideas and show curiosity in one another's work. The flexibility and creativity of the communal family group will derive from the deep implicit trust that members have for each other. No one will feel covetous or protective of their ideas or innovations.

There will be great freedom in the pace of labor as well; work teams will set their schedules, and on occasion report to the group. All this will be possible because trust has replaced hierarchy, and mutual understanding has taken the place of authoritarian commands. In the tractor factory or the furniture plant, everyone will have a part to play in research and design. Naturally, everyone too will be responsible for health and safety, for training and assisting the young, and for the few menial tasks that remain to be performed. Some people may choose to work at strange times or stay for longer hours, and the group will make every effort to accommodate their needs. Most people will work only half a day and devote the other half to education in the form of both teaching and learning.

Communal family groups are not only the wisest but the most economical way of living and working. Where everyone is both a worker and an owner living together in a family spirit, the level of trust and responsibility will be amazingly high. And where everyone knows they are cared for by the group, and that the group's well-being is identical to their own, work becomes an interesting challenge, not an onerous chore. It is reasonable to believe that illness, absenteeism, and employee mistakes will sharply decline. Work will strengthen people's intimacy with other members of the communal family, and their lives outside work will increase their creativity and efficiency in the workplace. In addition, work will be more efficient because the best labor saving equipment will be used. This will be done in an attempt to improve the quality of life for everyone.

In so many work situations today, labor and management

approach each other with cynicism, suspicion, and fear. The various departments of any business have entrenched interests in doing what is good for themselves, not for the company as a whole. In this atmosphere work has come to be the place where you rent yourself to the highest bidder for forty hours a week. Only one out of five Americans would continue working at their job, if he or she had the chance to retire.

Workers in a communal family have no need for the game playing that plagues most work situations. Information and assistance will flow quickly among them, while policing and supervision will shrink to virtually nothing. Since employees will be working for themselves, not the enrichment of remote corporate owners, the need for carrots and sticks will almost disappear. High-paid bureaucrats will become a vestige of the past.

Another incentive for people to invest in communal family living lies in the fact that it is rural. Almost everyone who is wealthy owns a farm or at least an estate in the country. This ought to tell us something about human longings. Everyone needs the exposure to land and nature that communal family living offers. Today, it is mostly the rich who have access to land. An investment in communal families is an investment in the good life for everyone, not merely the well-to-do.

For all these reasons, wealthy investors can find no better risk than a communal family business. The best shares in the stock market will return a pittance by comparison. By investing in a communal family, one is investing not only in products but in people and their families as well. And when wealthy people go further, investing some part of their lives as well as their money in a communal family, they will discover that living side by side with such people will be as enriching as the profit they reap. It should not be necessary to add that communal family businesses will never go bankrupt.

At the root of problems of investment is our nation's woeful lack of foresight. Investors chase the quick buck around the world and ignore long term needs. Communal families, on the other hand, live close to nature and to their children, so everything they do is rooted in shared collective needs. Different generations who coexist and learn from one another will create businesses that satisfy their own members, their surrounding communities, and the needs of the earth itself.

CHAPTER 11

Work as Self Expression

Many people, who have sought to carve out a new way of life in America in the last twenty-five years, have been in a state of rebellion against the work ethic. They see correctly that our competitive rat race mentality is unhealthy. Society has become divided into a class of managers or prodigals who work for selfish purposes and an underclass who work only because they have to. Many young people, often known as hippies, have experimented with alternative lifestyles which allowed them a quieter, more gentle life.

By rebelling against American Capitalism and its master-slave relationships, people lost sight of the virtues of the work ethic. This resulted from a fundamental confusion. In rejecting materialism and competitiveness, people also rejected hard work. They mistakenly believed that if it is wrong to try to spend one's life acquiring material possessions, then what went with it—hard work—was also wrong. Because there were so few models of hard work that were cooperative and enjoyable, people assumed that work itself was undesirable.

The work ethic needs to be understood in its original meaning. Work as it has existed in America has tended to be an attempt by individuals to accumulate as much wealth as possible. And one is supposed to do this by outsmarting other people, by exploiting their weaknesses and needs. Usually work is expected to be difficult and painful, a struggle to accumulate enough money to allow one finally to retire. Work is hardly ever in the service of community, or nature, or of one's own potential.

We need a new understanding of the work ethic. Work ought to be a way of fulfilling ourselves and making a meaningful contribution to the world. Through work we can explore reality in all its richness: its people, things, and natural wonders. Notice what often happens to people when they quit working, whether through retirement or unemployment: they become depressed and unfocused. People need a meaningful focus for their energies, whether it brings them a paycheck or not.

Work ought to bring out the best in people and make them feel energized and challenged. It should relate people to something larger and more transcendent than themselves, like furthering social justice, or better understanding nature and the cosmos. When work becomes these things, it enhances self worth.

One reason for our confusion about work is the perplexity widespread today about the nature of capitalism and its leading class, the entrepreneurs. What is important to understand is the essentially unethical attitude of anyone who tries to take advantage of another person's ignorance or foolishness in the marketplace. The taking of interest for example, was considered for centuries as the exploitation of another person's pain. But this does not mean that everything that happens in the marketplace is undesirable. The market is only as reliable as the personal honor and sense of fairness of those who participate in it. Perhaps the best thing a market can produce is ethical entrepreneurs who seek to do well by doing good. Underscore the word "ethical". America has a long history of unethical entrepreneurs—snake oil salesmen and people "selling water by a river." But there have also been many people who have genuinely fulfilled the entrepreneur's credo of finding a need and filling it. The challenge is to find a way to preserve what is ethical in entrepreneurs while eliminating what is dishonest and exploitative. Of course many goods, from health care to clean water, ought to be affordable by all, not doled out only to the few who can pay.

The ethical entrepreneur, instead of buying cheap and selling dear, offers the buyer a fair exchange, by producing something that truly enhances the quality of the buyer's life. In return, he receives capital, which enables him to produce more goods that serve society. The entrepreneur is the great source of creativity in a society and is to be highly valued as such. He meets a need that no one else meets, and in doing so, helps everyone.

The entrepreneurial spirit is essential for increasing our material well being. But there is no reason why it has to be selfish and unjust. People can take joy in using their creativity and spirit of innovation, not to make themselves rich, but to see that their fellow citizens live better lives. People can compete with themselves to further their contributions to society. In the society of communal groups envisioned here entrepreneurs would be highly rewarded not so much with money but with gratitude and praise. Entrepreneurs in such a society would make far greater contributions than are made today.

The lack of meaningful work or self employment that fits each individual's talents could be eliminated were we to initiate the free lifetime education which is called for by our instincts and planned for in the villages of communal family groups. At present our educational system leads to alienation and isolation which only makes human relationships more difficult and leads to the destruction of nature. This is a basic problem we must solve.

CHAPTER 12

Unity of People, Not the Chauvinism of Nations

In isolation we are physically, emotionally and morally weakened. When united and sharing with others we are confident and strong. A twig by itself is easy to bend, but fifty twigs bound together are far more than fifty times as strong.

It may seem like a paradox, but our individual power grows when we unite with others through consensus. Ten people working together as a group unified in thinking and feeling are much stronger and more effective than ten acting independently. The same goes for one hundred. The cables of the Golden Gate Bridge are made of thousands of strands of wire each of which separately is very weak, but when united hold a vast weight.

The Chinese speak of the Tao, a unity with all things that gives one great joy and strength. When we all become one with nature and one with ourselves we are at one with each other. In such a condition there will be no need for laws or states. Everything will flow naturally and productively.

Many nation states were spawned by empires and began as colonies. Their rule of law copied many things from their former masters, including oppression and taxes on the poor. Today nation states hide much of their actions from the citizens through spying on individuals and classifying as secret more and more government activity.

The boundaries of nation states are artificially created in the interest of controlling people and collecting taxes, rather than rational geographical or ethnic divisions.

Because the nation state is artificial, rarely does it trust its citizens. Many nations turn their weapons against their own people and nearly every nation keeps major decisions in the hands of the elite. When nations go to war, this distrust increases so that almost any dissent can be branded as traitorous. But since nations are nearly always at war, or on the verge of war, their own citizens begin to seem like the enemy. Spying on and policing one's own population becomes as important as fighting a foreign power. The development of nation states is as unnatural as raising rice on desert land. People who live in an area should be, like the flora and fauna, indigenous to the land. We need to dismantle the nation state and replace it with small self-governing societies.

Perhaps the worst expression of nationalism, short of war itself, is the idea of national service. National service, whether voluntary or conscripted, is an example of "might makes right." It allows the state with all its power to take over the lives of young people. But might can never make right, even when attempting to serve a higher end. Whether the government gets people to fight in a war or to serve the sick, it still is abusing its power. As long as we have national service of any sort, we are a step away from the draft.

Often the voluntary army is touted as a way for young working-class men and women to get a free education. But it is an education predicated on the notion "do or die and never reason why." Recruits must be ready to kill when their superior tells them to kill. This is a heavy price to pay for education. In fact the military credo "might makes right" goes against everything education stands for.

The path to the good life begins not with military schooling but with free lifetime education provided by communal family groups and financed by communal businesses, in agriculture, industry, commerce, and other fields.

Some day we will see an all-out contest between the free lifetime education provided by communal groups, and the free education advertised by our military establishment. Each offers help to the poor and an alternative to our decaying public schools. Yet one is democratic and constructive, the other authoritarian and dangerous. One is in the service of unity for humankind; the other disregards and will ultimately destroy all life.

Despite military power and the nation state, the path of evolution points to a society of free and equal persons living without hierarchy or greed. We see its foreshadowings today. Although many PhDs are as prodigal as corporate leaders, a growing number of students who achieve higher degrees have entered a world without hierarchy. In this world, reason instead of power prevails and decisions are made through consensus. Students of anthropology, psychology, or history can flourish here, for they have achieved the empathy and broad-mindedness which businessmen and politicians have not. They are aware of the values of other cultures, as well as the value and potential of oppressed groups within our own. They have learned to be judged on the merits of their thinking and writing, not by trampling over their rivals or pleasing the boss. And their number is growing. From these students will come much leadership for building villages of communal family groups.

CHAPTER 13

Animorality

More and more, human beings are beginning to grasp the fact that man is not the lord of creation, but only a piece within its puzzle. Yet for all our rising awareness, we still draw back in fear from the consequences of this view. Man is afraid to feel himself as merely one part of nature. He is afraid, most of all, that nature may have much to teach him—and that as an animal, he may need to learn from the other animals, those lowly brutes who arrived before him.

There is a deep morality in nature, a morality not always apparent to the casual observer. In nature everything is connected to everything else. Perhaps it is this sense of interdependence that is at the root of the conscience of nature. On some level nature strives to reproduce itself and moves towards states of increasing awareness and well being.

One of the greatest problems we face concerns the challenge of human morality. A caring society is not motivated by fear, either of God or the law of the state. Morality was once grounded in our love of nature. We lost this, and needed God to give us morality when we moved into cities and lost track both of ourselves and nature.

Part of the reason we see such crime in cities is because people there lose touch with the serenity and sense of perspective that nature gives. Nature gives people comfort and hope, and it is not surprising that without a strong connection to it people are prone to violence and crime.

Humans find themselves half in and half out of nature. We claim to be somehow "above" animals and in possession of a "higher" soul. But even a cursory look at the human species reveals that humans behave in ways far more abominable than animals.

Animals rarely kill other creatures except to get food. They don't engage in wars, commit murder for revenge, or perform any of the atrocities with which human history is sadly littered. It has been claimed that because humans are physically poorly equipped to do violence to each other, relative to other species, we have fewer inhibitions against violence. It is true that it is very difficult for one human being to kill another with his bare hands. Nature, in decreasing human inhibitions against violence, failed to take account of the human mind and its capacity to produce implements of destruction.

I am most impressed by the morality of animals when I think of the anecdotes I have heard about specific animals. The stories I hear about dolphins never cease to amaze me. In Florida there exists a place where, for a fee, humans can interact with trained dolphins. People can go swimming among them and get a powerful dose of interspecies communication.

One day a blind boy was brought to sit near the dolphins.

Because of his blindness it was considered unwise to let him cavort by himself among them. As he sat by the pool a dolphin who was known to be himself blind in one eye, nudged the boy into the water. He began gently guiding him around the pool to the astonishment of everyone present. After giving the boy a ride for awhile he nudged him back to the edge of the pool.

The story raises a number of questions that no one can satisfactorily answer. Did the dolphin know the boy was blind and feel a sense of kinship with him? If he knew, how did he know? Was he experiencing an outburst of love and compassion?

Animal trainer Ivan Tors tells a story that has been told many times about dolphins. He was swimming in a lagoon in the Bahamas and encountered a female dolphin who would eventually become famous for playing Flipper on television. Initially the dolphin snubbed him. Tors found that his scuba regulator was not working right, and as he surfaced to breathe he was hit by a seven foot wave that caused him to swallow at least a half gallon of salt water. He was hit by another wave and was on the verge of passing out when he felt the dolphin lift him on her back. He grabbed her back fin and rode to shore.

Examples abound in nature of animals showing a quality of love that humans can envy. One of the more astonishing ones concerns a hippopotamus, a crocodile and an antelope. During a drought an antelope came up to a water hole to get some water. As it drank a crocodile leaped out of the water and attacked the antelope. Seeing this a nearby hippo leaped on the crocodile's back and forced it to let go of the antelope who slowly moved away with its intestines hanging out of its torn belly. The antelope collapsed about thirty feet from the water. Then the unbelievable happened. The hippo came over to the suffering antelope and attempted to push its intestines back into its belly. It was of no avail; the antelope died in a matter of minutes. This incident was recorded on film and shows that even hippos can have the compassion to deliver first aid.

What are the lessons of all these accounts ? Moral behavior is of course related to intelligence, and as evidence mounts, it is clear that we have always underestimated the intelligence of apes, pigs, dolphins, and others of our animal forebears. Pigs, we now know, are able to care for and empathize with the needs of other species, and their memories are surprisingly good. Gorillas have mastered vocabularies of some 500 words, are able to speak in elementary sentences, and are being taught to transmit these skills to their young. Wild chimpanzees, like the ones observed by anthropologist Jane Goodall, demonstrate a great talent for using tools. But it is dolphins who, some believe, show the most astonishing mental powers of all.

One scientist who has worked with dolphins for fifteen years, a psychologist at the University of Hawaii, finds that their memory for sound easily outdoes man's. But more exciting is the dolphin's quick grasp of commands; within a year or so, the animal can learn to understand 100 words. Scientists are currently at work deciphering dolphins' own sonic language, which appears to include emotional signals (one rising-falling birdlike cry almost certainly means "help!") and even individual "signatures" that say "I am John Dolphin."

Alongside one of a dozen floating porpoise pens at Hawaii's Kaneohe Bay, biologist Earl Murchison plays an amazing game of twenty questions with a female bottlenose dolphin named Kae. Covering objects of various sizes in the water, he asks Kae questions such as "Is there anything out there? "Is it cylindrical? Is it metal? Is it moving?" Kae invariably gets her answers right, and each time is rewarded with a fish.

The mental acuity of dolphins is joined by what may be an advanced moral sense, although on this matter scientists are still divided. Through the centuries, the dolphin has been said to be an ally of fishermen and swimmers in distress. On some occasions an exhausted swimmer has reported being nudged toward shore; others have been brought to the surface to breathe, in the very way that dolphins rescue their young. Dolphins have also shown that they can learn to help themselves. For years fishermen have been learning to save porpoises from entanglement in nets, but as one ship captain observes, "The porpoises have been learning too. Nowadays when you put a school in a net, they just lie there calmly, saying, 'Hey, take it easy—it's just a routine we've got to go through.'" In some dolphin groups, a few of the animals will specialize in spotting fishing boats and warn the others of their approach.

The hierarchical instincts of animals brings our their compassion. But in humans, hierarchy opposes compassion. Humans may have instincts for hierarchy, but unlike other animals, we possess the ability to live in cooperation and consensus. With our big brains we must find ways to thrive through the natural consensus of groups.

CHAPTER 14

The Oneness of Life: Tao

The spirit in which people should live their lives is one that will one day make governments and laws unnecessary. It will generate trust among individuals and groups so that formal hierarchical structures will be unnecessary. The spirit in which people will live will be one that will collaborate with the energies of nature and not seek to dominate them.

This spirit was first written about by the Chinese sages some 2500 years ago. It is called the Tao. The Tao teaches us that all life is process and that we must be attuned, moment by moment, to the processes of life unfolding both inside and around us. By doing this we restore a state of oneness with both the natural and social world. It is such a state of oneness that I would like to see in communal family groups. Consensus, equality, and high productivity will naturally come about when people live in such a state of harmony. The fact is that most people are still at war with themselves and each other.

Such ideas may sound abstract and foreign to most Americans. Diane Dreher's book, *The Tao of Inner Peace*, gives concrete examples of what it means to live in the Tao. In any situation it is not what has happened but how we perceive what happened that is crucial. Dreher describes a situation in a hospital she worked at where a workman left a hot iron plugged in, filling the room with smoke. A doctor rushed in and demanded to know who'd made the mistake. Instead of solving the problem he was interested in affixing the blame.

Dreher talks about the difference between trying and doing. She describes an experiment where a man drops a pen on the floor and then tries to pick it up without picking it up. Then he simply picks it up. His point is that trying is only a half hearted attempt. Things that are important we simply do without needing to try. It is so much easier to take action than to think about taking action. The essence of the Tao lies in spontaneous action, grounded in a deep awareness of both one's self and one's environment. This awareness comes when we are able to balance the active, dynamic, or yang side of ourselves with the quiet, yielding Yin side. We must expect to live where we are at times intensely aggressive, and at other times soft and receptive. We must learn to be like bamboo: hollow and receptive inside, yet strong and graceful and able to bend with the wind.

CHAPTER 15

Return To The Natural World of Life

We are living in a dark age and only just now are awakening to the fact that we must end it or perish. It is the dark age caused by the two great revolutions, the Urban and the Industrial, which brought mankind off the farms and into the cities, out of close-knit families and into mass society, where individualism rules, empires control, and the needs of the family group are forgotten.

The Urban Revolution was the first great rebellion of prodigal sons. It began about 3000 B.C. in the fertile river valleys of the Middle East. Warrior-kings worshipping patriarchal gods turned their backs on family life, conquered the people of the countryside, and taxed them in order to build cities of wealth and luxury like Jericho, Baghdad, and Thebes. Whereas humans once lived in villages and governed themselves through family councils, now great urban capitals ruled over the countryside. These subjected peasants and their lands to the needs of kings, warlords, and priests. Dynasties such as Babylonia and Egypt conquered defenceless communities, and with their plunder created monuments like the pyramids and the ziggurats to glorify their name. Much of what we today label "religion" is in fact the megalomaniac expression of the urban empires. And much of what we study as "history" is merely the story these empires have written in praise of themselves.

The Urban Revolution has had deep and lasting effects on human society. It has shaped our beliefs and ideals in ways that we can scarcely imagine. In churches and schools (which are typical products of the urban age) we are told that civilization must come from the cities, and that a life close to nature is impractical and backward. We are told that masses of people and billions of dollars worth of technology are necessary to create a happy and comfortable life. We are given the message that central power is better than local self-government, big bureaucracies are better than families and small groups, and mass media are better than the pleasures people take in entertaining and informing one another. The Urban Revolution has glamorized politics, finance, and warfare—all of them the traditional business of rulers—and disparaged honest work that is close to the land and which serves ordinary human needs. We must reverse urban thinking before it gets too late.

The Industrial Revolution, beginning about 1800 in England and France, built on the achievements of the urban age but added some powerful and mostly destructive contributions of its own. Taking advantage of the concentrated population of the cities, and relying on government power, it unleashed a fury of machinery and manpower to exploit the air, water, and land. It banished whole peoples from their homelands and filled the countryside with smoke, noise, and waste. By ruling nature with an iron hand, men learned to exploit one another, to dominate women, and to repress the natural instincts within themselves. An unnatural civilization was created whose highest expression is the skyscraper—lonely, faceless, and disconnected from the earth and its inhabitants. Though modern man lives in crowded cities, loneliness plagues him more than ever before.

Yet there are signs of a new revolution. It is a revolution, slow and sometimes difficult to detect, that will take us out of the cities and suburbs and back to the land, where we will live creatively and harmoniously in villages of communal family groups. This revolution will have more impact on children and future generations than upon the innovators who are bringing it about. Yet its effects already are profound.

People are rediscovering their ancient bond with nature, their affinity for animals, flowers, and fresh air; for orchards and fields; and for honest labor performed in common with others whom they care for and trust. They are discovering that urban consumer society makes people more dependent, not more free. Most of all, they are discovering that families and friendships can thrive only within smaller communities, where there is communal parenting, employee-owned business and decisions made by consensus. From Vermont, to California, to Tennessee, these people are leading the post-Industrial Revolution.

Two profound effects of the new revolution may already be perceived. First is the deepening awareness of the interdependence of all things, an ecological sensitivity that is virtually a new religion. The children of our ecological pioneers will be as unable to live without closeness to nature as are we without TV, shopping malls, and movies. Second is the desire for new forms of leisure and work. The new revolutionaries are craftsmen, not mercenaries about their work; for them, work must be creative, meaningful, and useful for society. Leisure, therefore, becomes a part of work, not an escape from life or a form of recovery. In all these ways, the new revolution is returning us to the path of our instincts.

CHAPTER 16

Social Revolution Is Urgent But Is Long and Painful

Change from a highly competitive society to a cooperative one is a very difficult transformation. What this requires is nothing less than a revolution that will fundamentally alter our lives. Such a change, like the Industrial Revolution, may take several centuries but will eventually result in a cooperative society organized around communal family groups. The prodigals who own and run the government and corporations will have to relinquish their power.

If there is a single idea that must take hold of us, it is that we ourselves must take charge of our lives in every possible way. We must cease relying on substitute parents in the form of the government to change society for us. In a sense, human beings must finally grow up. This means not only ceasing to rely on government, but also learning to look at life from a long term perspective. The changes that need to happen will not occur instantly.

Prodigals, or goliaths, have been described but not their opposites, the Davids. A David is a person who regards life—his own and everyone else's—as precious, and sees that all life is deeply interconnected. Instead of being prodigal, the David is always frugal. He or she would never do something that offered short term personal gain which does not also provide long term benefit for others. The David combines a deeply felt awareness of the needs of the group with an intensely adventurous spirit.

If we can create a new kind of person who sees the world clearly, then change will occur almost on its own. No one can confidently predict how history will unfold. The problems that will arise at any given moment in the future are largely unrecognizable. But the attitude that must be taken towards these individual problems is clear.

Another characteristic of Davids is their toleration of pain in the interest of a larger struggle for good. The Davids view life as a grand adventure or experiment in which the goal is to work towards creating a world where everyone lives a meaningful life. Davids know that the world they wish to see may not come about in their lifetime, but they take great joy in the struggle to make it happen.

The Davids always think in terms of "we" instead of "I".

They are more concerned with the value of things than their price. They would never try to take advantage of someone else's ignorance for monetary gain. Davids will possess every bit as much energy and drive as do prodigals, but they will have a quality of gentleness and compassion that prodigals do not.

The challenge for men who are the new Davids will be to possess strength and energy without dominating others. The challenge for women will be to show equal strength without losing the capacity to nurture.

It will be necessary for the new Davids to unlearn many things that society has taught them. In American society every one is taught to think first of himself and to dominate others. With so many images of selfishness around us it will require work to produce a new kind of person.

We must let men like William Lloyd Garrison and Martin Luther King replace George Washington and John Rockefeller as American folk heroes. The new Davids will possess a completely new understanding of the past with a new set of heroes and heroines. When we create a new kind of person with new heroes, change will come more easily.

In future generations homelessness will end as communal housing grows. Gradually single-family homes will disappear, with their social isolation and costly waste of land. In their place will rise Mansion Houses for families of ten to twenty, located in villages instead of suburbs, and in an atmosphere closer to nature. Here human beings will begin to understand and value other living species.

These rural villages, which until now have possessed only farming and crafts, will begin to reach out and buy larger businesses which they can run for themselves. By pooling their capital and skills, and by putting to use the cooperative forms they have learned in family life, villagers will take over small corporations and set an example for the nation's future: a democratic, collectively-run industrial life. Efficiently run collectives may choose to invest their earnings in labor-saving techniques, in recreation and other amenities for their staff, or in ways of reordering work that may reduce its alienation and toil.

Future generations will begin to truly govern themselves. Communal villages, now experienced and secure and with years of practice in healing, will begin to care for the poor, the elderly, and the sick; for mental patients, unwed mothers, prisoners, juveniles, and all manner of the abused. Nurtured by strong and extensive family bonds, these individuals might become an asset, not a burden, in the diverse society that is under construction. Only incorrigible criminals will be left in the hands of the state.

Eventually the communal families will have the wisdom and experience to take over the commanding heights of the economy, and the state. Representatives from the villages will decide on a rotating basis the policies of national banking and the budget of the state. Experts will remain, but as consultants of the people and not its dictators. Every effort will be made to involve all villagers, even adolescents, in some decision-making process of at least regional importance. International affairs will be left primarily to professionals who will remain in constant and serious dialogue with the people. Much of the media will be publicly owned by individual villages or by networks of people with similar interests and needs. Education will become a very serious and lifelong task.

By the end of the next century, communal family groups will be the master and not the servant of their own economic and political lives. They will be free to turn to the realm of culture. Cultural centers within reach of the villagers will draw upon the advantages of rural life as well as the heritage of the cities, and establish museums, aquariums, science halls, opera houses and symphonies.

Education will probably fall under the control of the villagers. Young people will learn through appreticeships and by association with villagers at work and play. But formal schooling will become more coordinated with the informal education in the family and village, and the government will slowly lose control of the schools. Universities of higher learning will remain, pursuing research for the needs of the villagers as well as pure science and art. The role of the amateur scholar will come to flourish; there will be amateur historians and scientists as well as amateur actors, musicians and painters.

Population control will be a paramount historical task. People who are knowledgeable, powerful, and secure will not feed on the love of newborns nor conceive babies as a sign of adulthood or strength. Communal sharing and togetherness will sharply reduce the number of frustrated teenagers and unwed mothers, and instill the belief that parenthood is a tremendous responsibility even when it is performed by a group. Through education and contraception, and by alleviating poverty and stress, we can perhaps reduce the population growth rate, so that after several decades, our planet's population will actually commence to decline.

It will take centuries and many generations of change. But it will eventually bring us to a position of cooperation with nature and with our instincts.

CHAPTER 17

Creating Model Villages Across the Country

What follows is a plan for model villages of about 1500 people which will reconnect us to the wisdom of our instincts, instincts we abandoned ten thousand years ago. Life in these villages will be a challenge for everyone as we struggle to recreate for ourselves the harmony, autonomy, and security humans once experienced in communal groups.

Through a matriarchal role women give nurture and care to everyone. They take responsibility for rearing all the children and caring for the elderly and the sick. Man's role is to provide for the efficiency of the group, by putting labor and ingenuity into the factory and the farmland. Through model villages we can recover a peaceful relaxed life similar to the one that existed for hundreds of thousands of years before the coming of the Neolithic Era with its explosion of population and the beginning of military patriarchy.

Autonomy is envisioned as the animating spirit of the villages. This means, first of all, the freedom of everybody from unneeded authority—whether that of landlords and the banks which support them, or employers and supervisors whose priority is profit, not human fulfillment or creativity. Autonomy means, secondly, the spiritual growth that occurs through decision-making by consensus. Finally, autonomy signifies the development of young people in accord with their own potential. Through multiple parenting, and schools whose students teach one another, the young will grow up in their own way.

The people in this village will live in Mansion Houses where each communal family group of about twenty adults and eight or ten children will design and construct its own home. Within each home, members will design their individual rooms.

GROUP SIZE AND STRUCTURE

The size of the family group is very critical for the establishment of intimacy, which makes possible an automatic and natural consensus. Too small a number in the group makes survival difficult, as well as limiting richness and diversity, while too many people leads to alienation or domination.

Each village will require a plot of maybe 400 or 500 acres within a hundred miles of a city, central to the area. The general plan provides each individual adult a room which includes a 1/2 bath and approximately 250 square feet of space which they design themselves for their creative expression. Food will be stored and meals cooked in common areas. There will be a dining area where all house members can dine together and a smaller area where three or four can enjoy the companionship of more intimate meals. Planning these things will stimulate everyone's imagination.

A whole new attitude toward houses and indeed toward life will emerge because intimacy develops in this atmosphere. Members will come to see that their investments of time, energy, and money are really not investments for returning a profit but for life and creativity. And as people tailor their homes and apartment spaces to their individual personalities, they will no more want to sell them than they would sell their children or themselves. They will struggle to keep costs low to make the village economically feasible.

The village will be owned collectively. Its land will be owned by a nonprofit village association, who will be the stewards holding the legally recorded title to each Mansion House and a list of all adult members on a contract. There will be no shares of ownership that can be bought and sold individually, since assets will be communally held.

The village is intended for children of all ages, even the elderly, and the instinctual empathy of infants will be encouraged to flower. All village children will be financially assured of a free lifetime education. They will be expected to contribute to their communal family from age 14 to make them responsible members. Young people will help build, teach, garden, and make decisions affecting village life as soon as they show responsibility. In time there will be created a whole new kind of human being, a creature as different from us as we are from the Neanderthal man.

With proceeds from this book and the financial support of adventurous individuals and organizations that believe in shared ownership, these dreams can begin to take shape. Donations, grants and no-interest loans will also help. The sharing of ownership will bring members their greatest autonomy.

THE SCHOOLS FOR COOPERATIVE LIVING

To establish these villages, we would begin by creating Schools for Cooperative Living located perhaps in local schools or churches. They will be gathering places where recruitment begins for evening and weekend classes, in a two-year program that teaches how to create the model communities.

In these schools, ordinary people will find the confidence to stand up and challenge the society of the prodigals, and will pass on their confidence for the newcomers. It is as if a thousand Davids were to arise armed only with their ideals, and knock the Goliath of our present institutions off his heavy feet. Classes at the school will focus on the basic principles of design and construction. Other topics to be covered are carpentry, plumbing, foundation work, electric wiring, roofing and cabinet work. The classes will attract a diversity of adventuresome people, and set up a mansion house demonstrating the principles of the village to excite interest in the project.

It is anticipated that while several Mansion Houses may be built in the first few years, many years may be needed to complete the villages. But a detailed plan of the whole project will be drawn up to inspire everyone.

Liberal churches will be a natural ally of the villages and the school. Unitarians, Congregationalists, and others value education, communal living, and creative work, just as do the villages. The churches have the power and moral stature to persuade other Americans that communal villages are indeed worthwhile.

One-fourth of all Americans worship at a liberal church every week, making the churches an important form of moral education. No social movement in the past forty years, beginning with the civil rights movement, has succeeded without avid church support.

There are thousands of former Peace Corp volunteers everywhere who are looking forward to making a moral contribution to the world. Although many people feel frustrated that there are so few idealistic paths available, liberal churches offer one of the strongest sources of idealism.

Along with the technical program, concerned with housebuilding, there will be classes in group psychology, where students learn how to develop intimacy and fellowship among people of all social classes and ethnic backgrounds. They will learn how to recreate the proverbial American melting pot, as it were, only without the strife and mistrust that scars our history. People will discover that with growing intimacy and fellowship common decisions will be become easier to make.

In these classes, with the coming together of many kinds of people, prospective members can glimpse the radical changes required, when a portion of everyone's income is shared and decisions for spending are made by consensus.

If the income of the poor is to be pooled with the income of the rich, a major shift in understanding must occur. American society has, if anything, grown more competitive of late and people tend to trust each other less and less. This distrust has resulted in a powerful yearning to find a community where everyone feels like a family. Yet anyone entering a communal family group will be likely to feel certain fears and doubts. How can they be sure their fellow group members will be fair? Those with more money may have to give up old entrenched assumptions that their money entitles them to a greater voice than someone who possesses less. Poorer people will, in all likelihood, be faced with the opposite problem.

An important benefit for people living in communal family groups will be the experiences they have living and working with people whose lives have been radically different from theirs. So many privileged Americans have never truly been close to people who must struggle to survive. Real compassion will arise in people as they open their hearts to others who have been less fortunate.

The long two year orientation program will cause people to

confront these attitudes and to nurture the seeds of a new vision of social reality more concordant with life in a communal family. A few may conclude that they are unprepared for this long apprenticeship and transition. Can you imagine what effect living in this kind of village would produce in children from Harlem, South Africa, Bangladesh or Ireland?

ELEMENTS OF THE VILLAGE

Many different designs will emerge as members refine their skills and the Mansion Houses get built. But each house will need common areas for dining and house meetings. Much imagination will be needed to create dwellings that make communal multiple parenting as easy as possible and that provide the essential facilities for day care.

Other features of the village plan that will eventually be included are a school with a library, a farm, and busses for traveling. The school will be unusual in that everything the students do will be a part of the learning process to encourage their curiosity, including working on the farm.

It is hard to predict what the village school will look like, any more than the Mansion Houses or the ultimate layout of the village. But three features of the school will be significant and new. First, there will be a small farm with flower and vegetable gardens and an orchard. The farm will also have chickens, goats, sheep, pigs, and a variety of exotic birds including some that talk. There will be ponies, and of course dogs and cats. With help, the children might build the shelters and yards for the animals. The children will learn about the natural world by assuming the responsibilities suitable to their age.

Another important part of school life will be field projects. Busses will be available for groups of five to twenty kids to go on trips of various kinds, and learn firsthand about wood working, printing, weaving, camping, archeology and marine life. Led by adults, they will camp in the mountains and deserts, tromp through neighborhoods of the city, and possibly make themselves useful at a nearby farm.

A novel feature of the school will be the nature of its classes. They will consist of self teaching groups comprised of different ages, including even some parents or the elderly, and facilitated by a teacher or two. Segregating children into narrow age groups breeds boredom and conformity and will be avoided when possible. Some students might apprentice themselves to workers for a limited time, or to nearby farmers or craftsmen.

There will be classes for studying history and the physical and social sciences, in addition to ones in the history and practice of music and art. Most of all, competition will be replaced by group work and a spirit of common learning. Students will gain recognition for helping the groups and for ways they devise to increase cooperation. They will grade themselves, and sometimes grade the teachers. To the greatest degree possible, everyone in the community will be students and teachers at once.

Finally, the village will have space for a factory where, when it becomes large enough, perhaps half the adults will work in a community-owned business to provide themselves an income that is modest but secure. As the village grows in size and support, many opportunities will arise for an appropriate business or two, whether it be for production or services. It is important to keep in mind that a member of a communal family of twenty adults in the village will have more security in his communal investment than were he to own a $200,000 house mortgaged at 60% to a savings and loan. The whole group supports this person; whereas the isolated individual is prey to the menacing forces of the marketplace.

Self reliance will be the village aim for all its services with as little dependence on the county and state as possible. In California, this could begin with using solar energy where possible, recycling wastes, and training villagers in the rudiments of maintenance and repair.

Bibliography

Edward Andrews, *The People Called Shakers*

Johanna Angermeyer, *My Father's Island*

E.J. Applewhite, *Paradise Mislaid*

Hannah Arendt, *The Origins of Totalitarianism*

Ben Bagdikian, *The Media Monopoly*

Wendell Berry, *The Gift of Good Land*

Bruno Bettelheim, *The Children of the Dream*

David Brandon, *Zen in the Art of Helping*

Vine Deloria, *God Is Red*

Vincent Derlega, *Community, Intimacy, and Close Relationships*

Frans DeWaal, *Peacemaking Among Primates*

Marion Diamond, *Enriching Heredity*

Diane Dreher, *The Tao of Inner Peace*

Paul and Ann Ehrlich, *The Population Explosion*

Erich Fromm, *The Sane Society*

Marvin Harris, *Our Kind*

Harold Hayes, *The Dark Romance of Dian Fossey*

Charles Heiser, *Seed to Civilization*

Ivan Illych, *Medical Nemesis*

Carl Jung, *Memories, Dreams, Reflections*

Rosabeth Kantor, *Commitment and Community*
Sam Keen, *Fire in the Belly*
Clyde Kluckholn, *The Navajos*
Peter Kropotkin, *Mutual Aid a Factor in Evolution*
Richard Leakey, *Human Origins*
Michael Modzelewski, *Inside Passage*
Farley Mowat, *Never Cry Wolf*
Louis Mumford, *The City in History*
Natural History Magazine
Pierpont Noyes, *My Father's House*
Eric Raimey, *Shared Houses Shared Lives*
Susan Schaller, *A Languageless Man*
E.F. Schumacher, *Small is Beautiful*
Karen Schwarz, *What You Can Do For Your Country*
Philip Slater, *Wealth Addiction*
Sally Sontheimer, *Women and the Environment*
Garry Spence, *With Justice for None*
Olga Soffer, *The Upper Paleolithic of the Central Russian Plain*
Ivan Tors, *My Life in the Wild*
Margaret Wittmer, *Natural History; Galapagos Islands*